Mudpie Olympics and 99 Other Nonedible Games

St. Louis de Montfort
11441 Hague Rd.
Fishers, IN 46038

Contents

WHAT? ANOTHER GAME BOOK?

You had a lot of choices. You picked this book from a shelf of other game books. What are you looking for in *Mudpie Olympics and 99 Other Nonedible Games?*

Perhaps you were just curious to see what you could actually do with mudpies. Well, just turn to the first "crowd pleasing" event. You will find out quickly enough that you can make mudpies, decorate mudpies, or even judge mudpies. But please, do not eat them!

Perhaps you were curious to find out what other games you cannot eat. Many Christians are concerned about global hunger and have made a conscious decision to use food only to satisfy hunger, not in art projects or leisure activities. In *Mudpie Olympics and 99 Other Nonedible Games*, as in many other game books on the market today, we have chosen not to "play with our food." Unless food can later be eaten, such as in "Potato Pass" on page 27, we have chosen not to include it as part of this resource.

The Best of a Good Bunch

Did you have still other reasons for purchasing this book? Perhaps you just wanted a lot of games or something to help expand your own ideas. What are you going to do at your next gathering? How do you go about forming bonds through recreation?

If that is your need—or if you only want a few nonedible games after all—you picked out the right book! The games in this book are the best from the youth fellowship series *Directions in Faith*. That means that every one of these games works. They have been tried out by youth groups around the country, some of them for several years. *Mudpie Olympics* provides you with a few big events, designed to please large crowds; some ice-breakers; bonding exercises; relays and races; and variations on some old themes. There are even directions for enlivening an old (volleyball) game. Each of these one hundred games is a winner! Using them can help your youth group become a winning combination too.

Tried and True and Easy to Do

Having been youth group counselors ourselves (and some of us still continue in this role), we attempted to put *Mudpie Olympics* together in a "user friendly" way. With *Mudpie Olympics* you can:

- carry it around easily (convenient size)
- plop down and have it stay open (functional binding)
- follow the game directions (clear design, concise instructions)
- write your own notes about a game (lots of white space)

About the only thing we didn't do in *Mudpie Olympics* was waterproof it (which isn't a half-bad idea)! So, zip it in a sealable, clear food storage bag, if you are using it around mud, water, or other messy substance. Enclosing *Mudpie Olympics* in a waterproof bag will protect it for years.

What more could you want? Let us know! Our address and telephone number are included below. Perhaps you will see some of your ideas incorporated in a future gamebook! Meanwhile, have a great time!

Editor, Mudpie Olympics
201 8th Avenue South
P.O. Box 801
Nashville, TN 37202
Call toll-free 1-800-251-8591

BREAKING THE ICE

INTRODUCTION

**My memory is
so bad that many times I forget my own name!**
Don Quixote, bk.III, ch. 11, p. 195

Whether you are a small or large group, group bonding begins by becoming acquainted with each other. Begin with names! Here are some snappy, fast moving name games. When you have learned the names of your group members, use some of the other games in this section to become still better acquainted.

Use the white space below individual games to reflect on which ice breakers worked well and which you might want to revise to meet the needs of your group.

Zip-Zap-Zoom

• This game is best for groups of at least eight persons.

• Stand in a circle with "It" in the center.

• Each person has a "zip" (the person to the left) and a "zap" (the person to the right).

• "It" points to a person in the circle and says "zip" or "zap" and counts to ten.

• The person pointed to must name his or her "zip" or "zap" before "It" counts to ten or he or she becomes the new "It."

• As a variation, if "It" unsuccessfully calls "zip" or "zap" five times, he or she may call "zoom." Everyone in the circle exchanges places and the one left standing becomes "It."

Dollar Handshake

• This icebreaker is ideal for large groups, such as district-wide youth meetings, in which people do not know each other.

• Before the meeting begins, give one member a dollar bill. The person keeps his or her identity secret.

• During the meeting you will instruct players to shake hands with as many people in the group as they can.

• The fifteenth person to shake the hand of the person with the dollar gets to keep the dollar! Introduce the winner and the person originally given the dollar to the entire group.

• Variations: You may provide several dollar bills for larger groups so that more people will have the opportunity to win. Encourage donations to a favorite mission by putting collection containers for "Dollar Handshake" bills, coins, and checks near a gathering spot in the meeting room.

Move!

● Everyone sits in a circle.

● The leader calls out a description to move and a number of chairs to skip. Players who fit the description follow the instructions.

● For instance, if the leader says, "Move three seats to the right if you have red hair," persons with red hair would move to the third chair on their right, even sitting on the lap of the occupant if the chair is not vacant.

● Consult the following descriptions and add your own. Be creative when instructing participants to move.

Move _____ if you play high school basketball.
Move _____ if you are going steady.
Move _____ if you own a personal computer.
Move _____ if you have been to a rock concert recently.
Move _____ if you have seen the movie lately. (name a current hit)
Move _____ if you play in the band.
Move _____ if you are a straight A student.
Move _____ if you enjoy ice skating.
Move _____ if you ever had an embarrassing moment.

Human Bingo

● Have each player draw 16 squares on an 8-1/2-by-11 inch sheet of paper.

● In each square, players write a description of someone in the group without naming that person: a person with braces, a person wearing glasses, a female who knows an exchange student, a male who plays in the orchestra, and so forth.

● Collect the sheets of paper. Shuffle them. Pass them out again. Give each person a pencil.

● Then ask the players to get the autographs of persons who correctly fit the descriptions in the squares.

● As in the game of bingo, the first person to fill a vertical column is a winner. So are the first persons to fill a horizontal column, a diagonal line, all four corners, and the entire sheet of paper.

Who Am I?

● Pass a pencil and a three-by-five inch index card to each participant.

● Ask each to write five little-known facts about themselves on their card (where they spent their summer vacation in 1988, the name of a famous person they have met, their favorite hobby, and so on.) They should not write their name on the card.

● Collect the cards, shuffle, and redistribute them.

● Have each person read his or her new card aloud and try to guess who wrote it.

● If that person cannot guess correctly, give the other group members an opportunity to guess. Finally, ask the person who wrote the card to "confess."

● This game is good for smaller groups. It can help youth learn more about one another and discover common interests.

14

I Have Never

● Have the group sit in chairs in a circle with one extra person standing in the middle of the circle.

● The player in the middle completes the sentence, "I have never. . ." This statement must be true. For example: "I have never flown in an airplane."

● All persons for whom this statement is also true must remain seated. All players for whom the statement is false must find another chair in the circle, but may not move to an adjacent chair.

● The person in the middle tries to take one of the empty chairs, leaving someone else in the middle.

● The game then continues on with the new leader.

Duckie Wuckie

● Form a circle, with everyone sitting in chairs. Ask one person to volunteer to be "It." Remove that chair and blindfold him or her.

● After spinning "It" around several times, he or she must find someone in the circle, sit in that person's lap, and attempt to guess who the person is by listening to his or her voice.

● "It" will say, "Duckie Wuckie," to which he or she will respond, "Quack-Quack."

● Players may disguise their voice in any way they want, but they must respond.

● "It" will have three chances to say "Duckie Wuckie" (and three chances to hear a responding "Quack-Quack").

● At the end of that period, "It" will try to guess whose lap he or she is sitting on.

● If the guess is correct, that person must be "It." If the guess is wrong, "It" must go to someone else and continue the process.

Revelations

- Distribute index cards and pencils. Ask everyone to sit on the floor in a circle.

- Ask players to write down a fact about themselves that nobody else in the group knows. The fact might be a personality trait, a childhood memory, a grade, or a social security number.

- Collect the index cards, shuffle them, and read them aloud. After each fact is read, the group will try to discover who wrote it.

- The person who wrote the fact will attempt to wink at each of the other members of the group. When a person is winked at, he or she will say "It's not me" and will lie down on his or her back.

- The other players can guess the name of the revealer. If the guess is incorrect, the person guessing should lie down on his or her back. If the guess is correct, read the next fact.

- You may prefer to read all of the facts aloud, write them on the chalkboard or on a large sheet of paper, or photocopy them and give each player a copy. Then ask volunteers to submit to questioning from the group. The group is to ask each person five questions that can be answered yes or no.

- Then the group is to guess which of the facts he or she wrote.

Back-to-School Basics

● When group members return to school, give them a chance to hear one another's news in a quiz game.

● Divide the group into two teams, provide pencils and paper, and ask each member to fill in the blanks of a prepreared quiz that asks for general school information, like a favorite subject or activity.

● Either write the quiz on newsprint and post it where everyone can see, or give each team copies that you have prepared ahead of time.

● Appoint a captain for each team, and tell the captains to collect their teammates' quizzes and mix them up. Then have the captains exchange quizzes and pass them out to their team members.

● Next, alternate between teams, having one player at a time read aloud the quiz he or she has been given.

● Tell players to read only one answer at a time, pausing to give their teammates a chance to guess who wrote it.

● When a team guesses correctly, they score one point. If they guess incorrectly, they deduct one point. When all the quizzes have been read, add up the scores.

● Present the winning team members with apples. Offer to slice the apples in two and ask winners to share with the member on the opposite team whose quiz they read. Note that all members are winners because they've all learned something new about one another.

Four Facts/One Lie

● If you have more than eight people in your group, divide into smaller teams of five to eight players.

● Place the following categories on chalkboard or newsprint: my favorite child's game, my favorite musician or musical group, my favorite hobby, my favorite personality or hero, my favorite season.

● Go around the circle and allow each person an opportunity to answer these five questions. However, they should deliberately lie on one of the five questions.

● Players will have a chance to guess which answer was a lie.

Babes in Christ

• Have players bring pictures of themselves when they were young babies. The reverse side of each photo should contain the name of the person.

• Number the pictures and place them on a table. Give each player twenty to thirty seconds to identify in writing who each baby is.

• Borrow a few extra pictures from such people as the pastor, the youth leaders, and school teachers.

• Conclude the game by identifying each photo, letting the players keep score. This game leads nicely into topics dealing with growth as Christians.

Pass the String

● Invite players to cut a length from a ball of string. Give no further instructions.

● When all have cut their string, invite them to tell one fact about themselves for every time they wrap a portion of the string around their index finger. For instance, if the string will wrap around five times, players tell five facts about themselves.

M and M Pass

● Pass around a container of M and M candies and invite players to take as many as they wish (within reason!) and to hold them until all have been served.

● When everyone has received M and M's, instruct players to tell one true thing about themselves for every candy they took.

CROWD PLEASERS

INTRODUCTION

In all time of our distress,
And in our triumph too,
The game is more than the player of the game,
And the ship is more than the crew!
Rudyard Kipling, *A Song in the Storm*

One of the greatest challenges of any youth group is that of affirming the gifts and graces of each of those youth. When each individual feels celebrated, rather than discounted because of some lacking skill, a connection to the group is strengthened. Games, including multiple layers of games such as in these "crowd pleasers," are one of those "connectors."

Big, out-of-the-ordinary events help to create excitement in any youth group and often "please a crowd." Usually, there is something for everyone to do at these events and ways to affirm the interests and gifts of individual members, even if not everyone wants to get dirty or hit by a water balloon. Planning many small events as a part of the big event is one good way to "please a crowd"! Think of variety! Consider, and plan for, the individual needs of your group.

For example, is there a good organizer who might enjoy the planning or leading of events, rather than participating as a player? Can you use the photographic skills of a member who will get a kick out of filming the events? Have you an artist who might be affirmed by creating the invitations? You can "please a crowd" many ways, and in doing so, forge lasting connections among the various members of your youth group.

You may want to plan a "crowd pleaser" several times a year. Here are four events to get you started!

Mudpie Olympics

- Find a large, open area that you can wet down and make muddy, or save this activity for the day after rain.
- Tell players to wear old clothes and shoes.
- Have a water hose available to wash off the mud after the games are over.
- Divide the group into two. These teams can compete against each other for total points, but not all team members need to be included in all the games.
- Award prizes. Plan several games and relays for the group to play.
- Suggested games for the olympics follow.
- Make up your own mud games.

Three-legged Race

- Form teams of two. Players take off their shoes and socks. (This keeps clean-up time to a minimum!)

- Form "three legs" by tying the right leg of one partner to the left leg of the other or by putting those legs of each partner into a waist-high burlap bag or old pillow case.

- Instruct players regarding the particulars of the course. Instruct them to run, hop, or walk swiftly from point A to point B; teams that fall en route are eliminated from the race.

- Make the three-legged race more challenging by placing obstacles, such as old tires, in the race lanes.

Mudpie Touch Football

• Play like regular football, except that players "touch" the players in the opposing team, rather than tackling them.

• A "touch" is all that is necessary to stop the action. You may not be a lot cleaner, but at least you won't be eating as much mud as in the original version!

• Mark the parameters of your field by sticking yard-sticks into the mud, topped by a bright bandanna.

Frisbee Mudpie Football

• Play like mudpie touch football, except toss a Frisbee, rather than a football.

Grand Finale: Tug of War

• Be sure to conclude "Mudpie Olympics" with a tug-of-war in which the teams compete for twenty-five bonus points. Opposing teams stretch a rope between them, as individual team members grab hold of the rope in line. On signal, each team attempts to pull the other off balance into a water puddle or really muddy area.

Mudpie Pleasures

• Meet on the muddy banks of a creek or in a field after a rain and enjoy the childhood pleasures of mud!

• Provide pie tins or cake pans, little shovels, some sand in a bucket, colored pebbles, and so forth.

• Have each player make a personalized mudpie for another person in the group. (You might have them draw names for a mudpie exchange.)

• Afterward, encourage players to make another mudpie for a person of their choice.

• Grass or rocks add texture to mudpies. Leaves, small twigs, and shells make excellent decorations.

• Give prizes for the biggest mudpie, the most beautifully decorated mudpie, the slimiest, the most interesting, and so forth.

• Honor the cleanest person, the muddiest, and players who made the most pies.

• Let the pies bake in the sun while players play mud volleyball or go swimming.

Tator Night

- Don't be a vegi-tator or a hesi-tator, come to Tator Night! Make invitations in the shape of a potato and mail them in advance.
- Have everyone bring a "tator." Give a prize for the largest or most beautiful tator.
- Enjoy a tator taste-off. Place various kinds of chips in numbered bowls and let players rate the chips. Later announce the winner.
- Divide the group into smaller groups. Have each group create a skit or song. It could include parts like: Common-Tator, Medi-Tator, Dick-Tator, Agi-Tator, Emmy-Tator, or Cogi-Tator. Groups might be called the Hash Browns, Idahos, Scallops, or the Russets.

Potato Pass

- Divide into teams. Each team lines up, sits on the floor, and takes off their shoes. The object is to pass the potato from person to person down the line and back, using only their feet.
- The first team to get the potato all the way down the line and back wins.
- For supper, serve baked potatoes and let youth top them with bacon bits, broccoli, butter, sour cream, and whatever other toppings your group might like. Reduce expenses to the youth group by asking each member to bring his or her favorite topping from home.

Swimming Party

- Arrange for your group to have access to a pool for a swimming party. Plan an alternate date, in case of rain.

- Select a calling and planning committee to help organize the event.

- Invite an adequate number of adults to supervise, including at least one trained lifeguard to be on duty at all times.

- Plan water games and relay races that your group can play together: water volleyball, walking races at the shallow end of the pool, Frisbee games, relay races.

- Here are some other game suggestions:

Treasure Hunt

- For a treasure hunt, throw fifty pennies in the pool and have players dive for them.

- Always count the coins after the hunt to be sure nothing is left in the water.

- Be sure that having such small objects in the pool is not a problem for the filtration system or for other swimmers. Some public pools prohibit the presence of coins or other very small objects in the water.

Float Your Clothes

● Ask players to wear jeans and button-down, long-sleeve shirts over their swimsuits.

● Invite a Red Cross Lifesaving Instructor to teach swimmers how to disrobe in the water and how to use their clothing as flotation devices.

● Let players float around awhile on their clothes.

Apple Dive

● Put into the pool three apples for each player.

● Be sure that you have permission to put food in the pool.

● When you say "go," players should collect as many apples as they can and then swim to a designated place in the pool, such as the ladder or the diving board.

● Later wash and eat the apples at a pool picnic.

Musical Apples

- Put into the pool enough apples so that all but one player will have an apple.

- Be sure that you have permission to put food in the pool.

- As you play tape-recorded music, have players swim around the pool. When the music stops, each player should grab an apple.

- The person who does not have an apple must get out of the pool.

- Remove one apple and have swimmers play the game again.

- The game continues until you have only one player remaining in the pool.

- Wash and eat the apples as part of your meal.

- Close the party with a picnic. Have the organization committee arrange for group members to bring the food. End your swimming party with Christian music or a prayer circle.

Towel Mystery

- Ask each player to bring a towel in a paper bag.

- The bag should include some other clues as to the owner's identity. For instance, one person might include a brush, another a bottle of nail polish, and so forth.

- Place the paper bags, with a number written on each one, around the pool deck.

- Distribute paper and pencils.

- Players should guess who brought each paper bag. They may look at the towel and the other clues in the bag, and they may question each other, asking questions that require yes and no answers, such as "Is your towel a solid color?" They may not ask questions like "Is this your towel?"

- Players are to write down their guesses. After everyone has guessed, ask the players to identify their own towels.

- You might want to give prizes for the fluffiest towel, the biggest towel, the oldest, and so forth.

RADICAL RELAYS AND RACES

INTRODUCTION

To love the game beyond the prize.
Henry Newbolt, *The Island Race. Clifton Chapel*, st.2

Relay races are great for helping your group get to know one another better. Modify the races to fit the size of your group and the area you have to play in. Help everyone enjoy the games by heeding these points.

1. When dividing your group into teams, use a creative way to divide them up rather than having them choose teams. For example, divide by birthdays. The first six people born in the calendar year are on one team, then the next six, until all teams are formed.

2. Remember, competition is not the goal. Rather than looking for winners and losers, look for teams that are having lots of fun.

3. Since the object of the games is group building, everyone should participate in a way they find satisfying. Let them set up for or start the race. Others may want to photograph the hilarious results! Attempt to make your relays and races "user-friendly" to everyone in your group.

4. Food and water are frequently used in relays. Plan to use such items for a snack, following the game, rather than discarding them. If you cannot consume them, don't use them in a game. Raise the awareness level of your group. Discuss with them why food and water are too precious in a hungry world to waste.

Fan Relay

- Divide the group into teams, and have the teams line up single-file behind a starting line.

- Give each team member a blown up balloon and something to use as a fan, such as a record album cover. Give each team one uninflated reserve balloon.

- The first team to fan all its balloons in the air and across a finish line at the other end of the room wins. When a team member's balloon crosses the finish line, the next team member may begin.

- If a team member accidentally hits the balloon with the fan, or if the balloon hits the floor, he or she must stop and count to ten quickly before beginning to fan again.

- If the balloon pops, the team member holding the reserve balloon must inflate it, tie it, and hand it to the fanner. Teams popping all their balloons are out.

- Make sure that the fanner is not the person with the reserve balloon (unless he or she is the last member of the team).

- The reserve balloon is considered popped if the fanner inflates it. The only exception is for the last member of the team heading for the finish line.

- If the last team member pops the balloon, he or she must return to the starting line, inflate the reserve balloon, and begin again, just like any other fanner.

Make-up Relay

- Gather used containers of lipstick, eye shadow, blusher, and face powder.

- Have two volunteers (A's) sit in two chairs. Cover their shoulders and chests with towels. You may also cover their hair with shower caps.

- Divide the rest of the group into two teams, with one person (B's) from each team standing near one of the (A) volunteers.

- On the leader's signal, another member from each team runs to its (B) person and blindfolds him or her.

- Person (B) chooses one of the items of make-up in the collection, and attempts to apply the make-up to the face of person (A).

- When finished, (B) removes his or her blindfold, and another team member is blindfolded as new (B) and applies a new kind of make-up to the face of (A). The relay continues in this fashion, until each team member has had a turn as (B) and applied make-up to the face of person (A).

- The winning team is the first to have all its members apply items of make-up.

- Have on hand baby oil or cold cream to help remove the make-up (especially the lipstick, which doesn't wash off well) and a camera to preserve the results on film!

Shoe Find

- Form teams of five or six.

- Have the members of each team remove their shoes, put them in a pile, and mix them up.

- Then direct the members of each team to line up about ten feet from the pile of shoes.

- The first person in line will run to the pile of shoes and retrieve the shoes of the person who is next in line. He or she will put the shoes on the next person and run to the back of the line.

- Then the next person in line will run to the pile of shoes to retrieve the third person's shoes.

- When all the people on a team are wearing their own shoes, they should sit down.

- The first team whose members are seated wins.

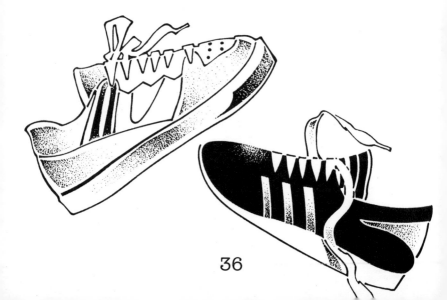

Shuck Them Duds!

• Divide the group into teams of five or six.

• Give each team a paper bag containing three or four articles of clothing. Pants, shirts, coats, dresses, socks, and shoes should be in large or extra large sizes. You might also want to include hats, ties (that must be correctly tied), or suspenders.

• Each person must put on all of the clothes in the team's bag, take them off, put them back in the bag, and pass the bag to the next person on the team.

• When the last person on the team has put the clothes back in the bag, he or she should shout, "We shucked them duds!"

• The first team to "shuck them duds" wins the race.

Skate Board Racing

• In this relay, each team has one skateboard.

• The object is to lie or sit (not stand) on the skateboard, cover a course (figure 8 or another shape), then return and tag the next person who does the same.

• The first team to complete the course wins.

Chariot Racing

● In this relay game each team of three has an old sheet to use as a chariot. The object is for one team member to sit on the sheet and hold on tightly while two other team members pull the chariot around the course.

● You determine the shape of the course and how many times each team of three must complete the course.

● When they return, the next group of three goes. This continues until a predetermined number of groups of three have gone from each team.

● If you do the relay outdoors, you may want to substitute old pieces of tarpaulin, heavy cardboard, or heavy material for the sheets.

Nondividing Amoebae Races

- Divide into teams of six members.

- Have five of the six team members make a circle with their backs to the center. Have them hook their elbows together.

- Have the sixth team member get in the center of the circle.

- Have all teams line up on the starting line in this manner. When you say "go," they are to run to the turnaround line and back.

- The first team to go down and back without their amoebae dividing wins.

Backwards Relay

- Divide the group into teams of four or more people.

- Mark a course for the event, including a starting line, a finish line, a turn, and perhaps one or two obstacles.

- Explain that each person on each team will complete the course doing a different activity backwards. For example, the first person on each team might run backwards, the second will crawl backwards, the third will hop backwards, and the fourth march backwards. Be creative!

- The first person on each team must complete the course before the second person begins.

- The first team to complete the course wins.

Blind Leap Frog

● Add a new twist to an old game! Mark a starting line and a finish line. Make the lines parallel, or make them perpendicular and add a turn to the course.

● Divide the group into teams of four or five people. Invite the members of each team to line up single file behind the starting line; then blindfold them. Signal the relay to begin. Teams are to race to the finish line, playing leap frog.

● This game requires that participants communicate. Be sure someone is watching each "frog" so that no one gets hurt.

Charades

• Write instructions such as "neigh like a horse," "flap your wings like a bird," "spin around," "take your shoes off," or "quote John 3:16."

• Each instruction should be on a separate sheet of paper, and the sheets of paper should be folded so that instructions are hidden.

• Divide the group into two or more teams. Each team will have an equal number of turns.

• About ten feet in front of each team, place a bucket containing an equal number of instructions for everyone on the team.

• Begin the game. The first person in each team runs to the bucket, pulls out a set of instructions, reads them, pantomimes what they say, and returns to his or her team. Then the next person takes a turn.

• The first team to empty its bucket wins.

Balloon Golf

- Place masking tape in a long line across the floor in one section of the room.

- Form two equal teams and have them face the line.

- Give each player a balloon, with all members of the same team having the same color balloon.

- To tee off, the first player for each team blows up a balloon (do not tie a knot) and lets it go in the general direction of the line. Then he or she runs to the spot where the balloon landed, blows it up, and lets it go again.

- When the first player successfully gets the balloon across the line, he or she runs back and tags the next player on the team.

- The first team to have all its players get their balloons across the line wins.

- Variation: ask each player to count "strokes" (the number of times he or she has to blow up the balloon before it gets across the line) and the team with the fewest strokes wins.

Straw Relay

- In this relay game each team has a one-gallon jar of water on a table in the center of the room.

- The teams are positioned at an equal distance from their water.

- Each team member has his or her own straw.

- The game begins with the first member of each team going to the jar and sucking as much water as he or she can in the time limit.

- When time is called, the player turns back to tag another member of the team who repeats the process.

- The key to this game is to vary the time allowed at the jar. Vary times from five seconds to a full minute.

- The first team to successfully empty the jar wins.

Apple Paring Contest

- Give each person an apple and a sharp knife. When instructed, participants begin to pare their apple.

- The person with the longest length of apple skin is the winner.

- For larger groups, divide into teams and give each team one knife.

- The members of the team take turns paring the apple, and the team with the longest single length of apple skin is designated the winner. This game takes patience, skill, and luck.

- Eat the apples for a snack.

Blind Banana Feed

- Divide the group into pairs.

- In this game one person is blindfolded, and the other player's hands are tied behind his or her back.

- The person who is blindfolded peels the banana and feeds it to the person whose hands are tied.

- This can be done in couples or as a relay.

Bubble Gum Relay

- Form at least two teams and line up in a relay race fashion.

- The first person in the line begins the relay by receiving a piece of gum.

- He or she opens and chews it until he or she can blow a bubble.

- That person must then run to the supply table at the other end of the room and bring back an item for the next person.

- Some suggestions for items include: 1) three crackers to eat and then try to whistle or 2) two marshmallows or cereal to toss up and catch in your mouth and then eat (one at a time).

- Alternate these items to finish the relay.

Body Flossing

• This is a relay contest between two or more teams.

• Each team must tie a line, a piece of yarn, or a string to a spoon and drop the spoon down the shirt of one member, up the shirt of another member, and so on until the floss is threaded through the shirt of each member of the team.

• Announce (somewhat belatedly) that the relay is not over until the spoon is reversed and returned to the first person in line.

• Variation: Chill the spoon beforehand!

VOLLEYBALL VARIATIONS AND OTHER SWEATY STUFF

INTRODUCTION

"The game is done! I've won, I've won!"
Quoth she, and whistles thrice.
Samuel Taylor Coleridge
The Rime of the Ancient Mariner
pt. 1, st.12

Volleyball is an age-old classic. Youth and adults alike enjoy this competitive game. However, some people are not as skilled in competitive games as others are. Some may be afraid of being hit by a ball—or being kidded about how inept they are.

What's the answer? Change the rules! Change even the equipment! Use the following suggestions to even the odds a bit!

Noncompetitive Volleyball

● Set up a net and provide a ball for a game of noncompetitive volleyball.

● To determine teams, have players line up in alphabetical order and divide the group in half.

● If your group is large, you may want to use more than one net, or have several rounds, or agree on a number of points for a shortened game.

● Although the teams keep score, everyone will be a member of the winning team because all players will rotate to both sides of the net.

● The rotation can be done in a large S or squiggle shape. Both teams move when the ball changes sides.

Drop Volleyball

● Play a regular game of volleyball with a couple of rule changes.

● The ball must bounce once before the returning team can touch it.

● Teams have an unlimited number of hits to get the ball back over the net as long as the ball does not hit the ground again.

● Repeat this procedure every time the ball crosses the net.

Blind Volleyball

● Place a blanket over the net, so that the players on one side do not know how the players on the opposite side are serving.

● This variation works well for either regular volleyball or water balloon volleyball.

Balloon Volleyball

● This game is played like volleyball, except that a large balloon is used instead of a ball.

● One person begins the game by batting the balloon over the net.

● Keep the play close to the net in order to keep the balloon aloft.

Sit-Down Volleyball

● Tell everyone to sit on the ground (they cannot raise off the floor), lower the net, and play with a beach ball or a Nerf ball.

● This variation eliminates the element of spiking and keeps players from hogging the ball.

Water Balloon Volleyball

● Form two teams of an equal number of players. Each team holds a double sheet, taut, among them.

● Place a water balloon in the center of one team's sheet.

● Working cooperatively, the team catapults the filled water balloon over a volleyball net. The opposing team attempts to catch the hurled balloon in their sheet.

● Play continues until one team is unsuccessful in catching the unbroken water balloon.

● Points are scored as in regular volleyball.

● When a balloon breaks (and many will), simply supply a new, filled water balloon.

● The game is over either when the supply of water balloons has been exhausted or one team has been awarded 21 points.

Broom Hockey

• This game is best done in a carpeted room or on a piece of carpet.

• The playing area is shaped like a rectangle with a goal box marked at each end with masking tape.

• Divide the group into two teams. The two teams sit on the two long sides of the rectangle.

• Tie a knot in a rag and place it in the center of the play area. Place two brooms on the floor.

• The members number off so that the two number one's are at opposite ends of the play area as goalies.

• The game leader calls a number. If the number is three, the three's from each team will get up, grab a broom, place one hand over the tip of the handle, and try to sweep the rag into the opponent's goal.

• If a player removes his or her hand from the top of the handle, the opposing team can win a point automatically by shouting the word "handle."

• The handle rule protects the players from getting hit with a broom handle.

Shuffle Your Buns

• Place enough chairs for each participant in one large circle. Have each person choose a chair. Select a leader to stand in the middle of the circle, leaving one empty chair.

• The object is for the leader to sit in the empty chair.

• If the leader manages to do so, the person sitting on the right must go to the center of the circle and try to return to an empty chair.

• Players try to prevent the leader from sitting in the empty chair by sliding to the left whenever the chair beside them is empty. (The entire group is shuffling in a clockwise direction in an attempt to keep the leader from sitting down.)

• For added confusion and excitement, add the element of change. Announce that the rules (and the direction of the circle) change whenever you blow a whistle. If the group is moving clockwise when the whistle is blown, whoever is sitting to the left of the empty chair is in danger of being caught. The group then rotates in a counterclockwise direction.

Anatomy Shuffle

● Ask all the members of your group to stand in the center of the room. The leader may choose to be a participant as well.

● The leader calls out two parts of the human body (arm-kneecap, forehead-elbow) and everyone scrambles to find a partner and match up the appropriate body parts (use only one pair, such as one arm to one kneecap, and don't embarrass anyone).

● After everyone is linked to a partner, you may want to make the game more interesting by having each person tell his or her partner about something that happened this week.

● Call out two more body parts, give everyone time to find a partner, and again tell something that happened this week. Continue to enjoy this game together.

The Number Game (Fast Version)

- Ask group members to sit in chairs in a circle and number off, beginning with No. 1.

- It might be helpful to have everyone write their number on a piece of paper and to tape it to the inside of their chair. The number belongs to the chair, not the person.

- As persons move from chair to chair, their number changes.

- The person who has the largest number is the caller. The caller will call out any number except his or her own number.

- The person whose number is called has one second to call another number.

- If players make a mistake, they must go to the bottom of the group (the chair with the largest number) and become the caller.

- Everyone below the caller moves up a chair.

- The object of the game is to work your way up to chair No. 1.

Train Wreck

● Place a row of chairs in a straight line, one behind another. You should have one chair less than people in this game.

● Each person numbers off from one to the total number of participants. Players keep these numbers throughout the game. Everyone takes a seat. The last person is the conductor and stands in front of the group.

● The conductor calls out any series of numbers (using no number higher than the number of participants), after which he or she announces, "train wreck!"

● That phrase is the cue for the conductor and each person whose number was called to change chairs. The person whose number was not called remains seated. Whoever is left standing after everyone has changed chairs is the new conductor.

● That person moves to the front of the line and calls out a new set of numbers, followed by "train wreck!"

● Larger groups will want to form several lines, with approximately the same number of chairs in each line. In this case, however, the leader will call out the numbers, and players will not be allowed to change from one row of chairs to another.

Fast Food to Go

• This fast-action game is designed for six or more players.

• To begin the fun, have all but one of the players sit in chairs in a circle. Leave enough space between each chair to allow participants to move freely between them.

• Each player is given the name of a fast food—hamburger, hot dog, cheeseburger, fries, and so forth.

• One player stands in the center of the circle. The person in the center calls the names of two or more fast foods.

• When players' foods are called, they must get up and change seats. The caller will also attempt to find a seat.

• The person left standing goes to the center and becomes the caller.

• If the person in the center of the circle calls "fast food!" all of the players attempt to change seats.

• The activity continues until the group is ready to stop.

• If you have twenty or more players, number off to four or more and give each number the same food (for example, all the ones are hamburgers).

Skateboard Jousting

- In this game two teams compete against each other by jousting.

- Secure a skateboard (the bigger the better) and a large pillow for each team. Participants sit on the skateboard.

- The first players of each team propel themselves toward each other and joust with pillows.

- Knocking the other person off the skateboard scores a point.

Birthday Blitz

- Players sit in chairs in a circle. Have one less chair than people.

- One person starts out standing in the middle of the circle. That person calls out two months in the year.

- Anyone who has a birthday in the months called stands up, runs to a chair left vacant by another person, and sits down. At the same time, the person in the middle tries to sit in a vacant chair.

- The person left without a seat then goes to the middle and calls two more months.

- When the person in the middle yells "Birthday Blitz," everyone has to get up and find a new seat.

Musical Guys

● All the guys form a circle, facing toward the center, on their hands and knees. The girls form a circle on the outside of the guys' circle.

● Play some music on a tape player. When the music begins, the girls walk in a clockwise fashion, just as in the game "musical chairs."

● When the music stops, each girl must try to sit on the back of one guy. The girls who do not accomplish this goal are out of the game.

● Before round two, remove one or two of the guys from the circle.

● Girls walk as before, grabbing a guy when the music stops. Continue until all have been eliminated.

Dodge-a-Sponge
(Outdoors)

● Place four or five five-gallon buckets around the perimeter of a circle.

● Fill each bucket halfway with water and drop a large sponge into each bucket. All players are in the circle. Only the leader is at the perimeter of the circle.

● The game begins by the leader throwing a sponge at someone. The person the sponge hits must join the leader at the edge of the circle and begin throwing sponges also.

● The game continues until only one player is left in the circle. That person is the winner!

● Throwers can retrieve sponges that drop inside the circle, but they must dip the sponges again before they throw them.

Blind Ambush

- Form two equal teams. Number off, making sure each team has a player for each number. Each player needs a blindfold.

- Form a circle with everyone sitting in no particular order. Place a squirt gun in the middle of the circle.

- Call a number at random. The two players with that number put on blindfolds and go to the middle of the circle to hunt for the squirt gun.

- The player who finds it cries out, "Got it!" and tries to squirt the other player.

- However, the other person tries to get back to his or her place in the circle before being squirted.

- If the player with the gun squirts the other player before he or she returns to the correct place in the circle, his or her team gets a point. If the player returns safely, that player's team gets the point.

Marco Polo by Land

- Remember playing "Marco Polo" in a pool? Here's a variation that requires water balloons.

- Set boundaries in a grassy area outdoors.

- One person, armed with two water balloons, stands in the middle of the designated area.

- The other participants scatter around the area.

- The person in the middle is blindfolded and counts to five. During the counting, everyone can move.

- After counting to five, only the blindfolded person moves. He or she says "Marco," to which the others (standing still) reply "Polo."

- The person with the balloons can call out "Marco" one more time, trying to locate one of the other players.

- If "Marco" thinks he or she has pinpointed a "Polo," "Marco" is allowed to throw a balloon.

- If "Marco" misses, he or she begins with the count again. When "Marco" gets a hit, that "Polo" becomes a "Marco."

Indoor Snowstorm

● Secure as many old newspapers as possible.

● Designate a line down the middle of the room and form two groups, one on either side of the line. Give each group an equal number of newspapers.

● For three minutes, each group tries to get as many newspapers as possible on the other half of the room while trying to keep their own half free of newspapers.

● The players may wad the newspapers and throw them, or they may wad the newspapers and shove them over the line in piles.

● Nobody may step over the line, and no physical contact may be made between players on opposing sides of the line.

● When time is called at the end of three minutes, the groups fold the newspapers on their side for recycling and take them to a recycling center later.

● For an added twist, designate a colorful section of newspaper (perhaps the comics) as "slush." The group that has the "slush" will be last in line for refreshments.

Bedlam

- Divide into four teams (using birth dates is a good way to form teams) and send each team to separate corners of the room.

- The object is for each team to race to the opposite corner of the room and sit down.

- The first team to reach the opposite corner wins that round. Naturally, everyone will meet in the middle of the room and cause bedlam!

- In Round 2, change the rules. This time have everyone run backward!

- In Round 3, instruct each team to hold hands while they run.

- Try crab walks, fire fighter carry, skipping, or any other method you may think of.

Clumps

- This game is a great way to help youth mingle and allow "safe" touching.

- Start by instructing the entire group to stand in the center of the room. Tell them to move around at random.

- Call out any number. Everyone should then scramble to form "clumps" consisting of that number. When the clump is formed, sit on the floor.

- After all clumps have been formed, ask everyone to stand and mingle again. This time call out a different number and repeat the process.

- Option: Instead of calling out numbers, bang a kitchen pan with a spoon. Participants should form clumps consisting of the same number of people as taps on the pan.

- This game is a good way to divide teams for discussions or competition.

Line Up

● Divide your group members into teams with an equal number of players on each team. The larger the teams, the better.

● Each team competes against the other teams to see which can line up in a straight line the fastest.

● You will announce the criteria by which each team is to line up by using the following suggestions and/or adding any that you can think of.

● For even more fun, play this game blindfolded.

● Line up according to:
  Height (tallest to shortest)
  Age (youngest to oldest)
  Alphabetical order by last name
  Birth month
  Alphabetical order by first name
  Shoe size (smallest to largest)

Two Ankle Stomp

● Form two teams. Each person is given two balloons and two four-foot lengths of string.

● Each person blows up the balloons, ties them off with a knot and the string, and then ties the string to his or her ankles so the balloon is about three feet away from the ankles.

● Each team should have its own color of balloons.

● The first person from each team goes to the play area and when the game begins, he or she will try to stomp the balloons of the other person, while protecting his or her own balloons.

● A person is eliminated when both balloons have burst.

● The last person in gets the points for his or her team.

● For the next round, the second person from each team goes out, and so on.

Bunny Hop Pop

● Before the group plays, blow up several balloons. The larger the group, the more balloons you need.

● Instruct the members of the group to scatter the balloons on the floor in the center of the room.

● Divide the group into teams of at least four, ideally six, people. Each team will start from a corner of the room.

● Instruct the members of each team to line up single-file and to put their hands on the hips of the person standing in front of them.

● When you say, "Hop," the teams will hop to the center of the room and pop as many balloons as possible by stomping on them.

● The first person in each line may not pop any balloons; he or she should keep track of the number of balloons his or her team pops.

● The team that pops the most balloons is the winner.

● Play suitable bunny hop music. Make the game more challenging: blindfold the leader of each team.

● In warm weather, play "Bunny Hop Pop" outside and fill the balloons with water.

Balloon Toss

● "Balloon Toss" is especially nice on a hot, muggy summer afternoon. The game is played like an egg toss.

● Ask the members of the group to find partners. Give each pair a water balloon.

● The partners are to stand about seven feet apart, facing each other.

● One person in each pair is to toss the balloon to his or her partner.

● If the toss is completed successfully, both partners take one step backwards and attempt another toss. The last pair to complete a toss without breaking the balloon wins.

● Of course, the real excitement comes when balloons break and players get a quick shower!

"BANDED TOGETHER" AND OTHER BONDING GAMES

INTRODUCTION

Play up! play up! and play the game!
Sir Henry Newbolt, *Vitai Lampada*

One of the advantages of playing games is that people have a way of coming together through play! Play really does serve to "connect" persons who otherwise might have little in common. While some games of the past focused on the abilities of the few (while others cheered from the sidelines), there are many games that can effectively involve your entire group. As you discover the games in this section, encourage leadership to emerge. There are no captains in these games, no assigned leaders—but rather leadership tends to emerge as a task is attempted. Some of your quieter members may shine, drawing upon skills that may have remained hidden in more traditional games of "winners and losers."

Perhaps you will discover, as have others, that your group has become a community of winners as players tackle some of these "banding and bonding" opportunities!

Banded Together

● Before the game, hide a treasure somewhere in the room. The treasure might be a bag of homemade cookies, coupons for fast-food, or free passes to a movie. You should also write one or two clues hinting at the location of the treasure.

● Divide the group into teams of at least five.

● Give each team member two medium-sized rubber bands. Each player should connect the rubber bands and put one around his or her ankle and the other around the ankle of another person on the team.

● When a team is banded together, each player should have one rubber band on each ankle and should be connected to two other youth.

● Explain that a treasure is hidden somewhere in the room and that you will read one clue to its location.

● As soon as a team thinks they know where the treasure is hidden, they should start moving toward it.

● Let the teams know if they are moving closer or farther away from the treasure.

● If one person breaks a rubber band, the whole team must stop until it is replaced.

● The team that finds the treasure first wins. Follow this game with some discussion on how you perceive your group to be "banded" together.

T-Shirt Tower

● Place a clean T-shirt on the floor. The object is to see how many people you can stack on top of the T-shirt.

● No one may touch the floor with any part of the body.

● This game requires creativity by the group to determine where to place each person. Try sitting on one another's shoulders, forming a pyramid, or climbing on someone's back.

● If you have a larger group, divide into smaller teams and compete to see which team can successfully stack the most people on the T-shirt.

Ooh-Aah

- Have players stand in a circle, holding hands.

- The leader begins by squeezing the hand of the person on the right and saying, "ooh." That person squeezes the hand to the right and repeats the phrase. Continue around the circle in this fashion.

- When the leader chooses, he or she squeezes the hand of the partner on the left, saying, "aah." That person squeezes the next hand on the left, saying, "aah," and continues around the circle in this fashion.

- The meeting of the two (ooh and aah) in the middle produces an hilarious moment!

Circle Sit Down

● This noncompetitive game is great for groups of eight to eighty-eight.

● Form a large circle and have everyone face toward the center.

● Have each person turn one quarter of a turn to the left, facing in the same direction (counterclockwise).

● Then take a side step toward the center of the circle. Each person should now be facing the back of the person in the front. This move provides a good opportunity for the entire group to rub one another's shoulders.

● Now your group is prepared for the "circle sit-down."

● At the count of three, everyone should sit slowly on the lap of the person behind.

● Hold that pose for a few moments and then tell everyone to stand up slowly.

● If your group does not successfully sit down on the first try, attempt it again.

● For variety, have everyone turn around and face the opposite direction. Then again instruct them to sit down.

● This game incorporates teamwork, touch, and excitement in a noncompetitive way.

Knots

- Have the group stand in a circle.

- Each person is to reach across the circle and take the hand of two other persons. When all hands are held, the players will form a human knot.

- Players untie the knot by turning around and going under the connecting arches of arms.

- No one should let go of one another's hands until the human knot is completely untied and they are standing in a circle.

I-Machine-Ation

● Divide into teams of four to six people.

● Ask each team to prepare a human machine, using a person as each of the parts of the machine. Each part is to be a moving part.

● The whole machine may be a model of a real machine or a crazy new team invention. Examples: airplane, pencil sharpener, washing machine, beach umbrella.

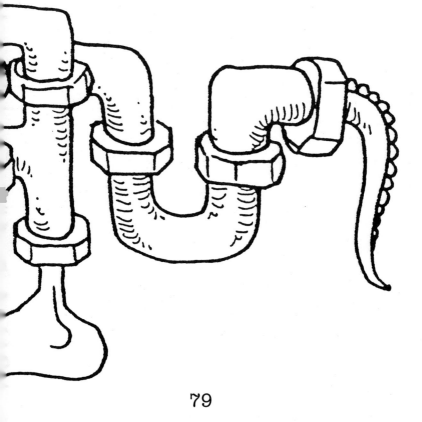

Circle Back Rub

● Sit in a circle on the floor. Then have everyone turn to his or her left (or right) so that each person is facing another person's back.

● Then each person is to give a back rub to the person in front of him or her.

● Suggest that players use various techniques: rubbing, patting, chopping with the sides of their hands, kneading, using their fingertips or the heels of their hands.

● You might also suggest that players sing as their backs are being rubbed. Raising or lowering their voices will make interesting sound effects.

● After a few minutes, have everyone turn around and massage the back of the person who is now in front of them.

Cinnamon Roll Up

• Tell everyone to hold hands in a circle, facing toward the center.

• Ask one person to drop the person's hand on the right and to begin to spin in a counterclockwise direction into the circle. This action should cause the rest of the group to wrap around the spinner (much like a large cinnamon roll).

• Tell everyone to give the group a big hug and then let go.

• This activity is a nonthreatening way to help your group physically touch one another.

Hug Relay

● You can create great new games by combining two or three other games. "Hug Relay" is a combination of other well-loved games. Begin by dividing the group into teams.

● Play the game "relay style" with each person taking a turn being a "runner."

● Explain that you will call out a characteristic (or several) and that runners should attempt to find someone on another team who possesses that characteristic.

● The first runner to find that person, give him or her a hug, and return to his or her team wins a point for that team.

● After several rounds, total the points and congratulate the team with the winning score.

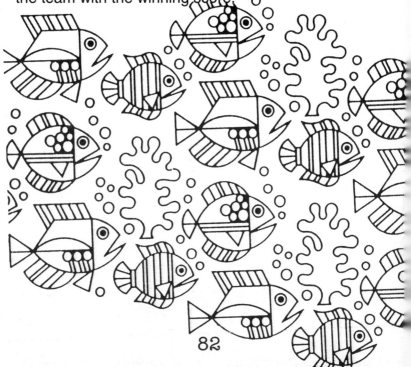

Sardines

- This is group "hide-and-seek."

- Choose someone to be "It," and ask "It" to hide while the group counts to 100.

- The group begins counting in whispers, gradually increasing in volume until number 100, when reached, is shouted.

- Next the group separates to search for "It." (If outside after dark, travel in pairs.)

- When a person finds "It," he or she hides with "It," keeping very quiet. Each person who finds "It" stays in the hiding place with the others.

- Eventually, there will be just one person searching, and the remainder of the group will be with "It," packed in like SARDINES!

- The last one to find "It" (and the rest of the fish) becomes the new "It," and the game begins anew.

Photo Scavenger Hunt

- For a really wild evening, try this variation of the old scavenger hunt game.

- Divide into teams and give each team an instant camera with film and a list of places or situations where they must take a group picture. No two lists should be the same.

- Each player should wear a name tag identifying him or her as a member of your group. Wearing tags helps gain the cooperation of persons in your community.

- Set a time limit (usually 45 minutes or one hour) for the teams to complete their lists.

- When they return, share pictures, laughs, and stories. Save the pictures for your group's scrapbook.

- Some situations for group pictures might include the following: with police or fire fighters, in a phone booth, in a new car at a dealership, bagging groceries at a supermarket, making a human pyramid in front of city hall (or the courthouse), inside a bathtub, going down a slide, gathered around a tombstone from the 1800's, with a nurse in uniform, saluting an American flag, servicing a car at a gas station, walking like a line of ducks across an intersection.

- The key to the game, of course, is not taking the pictures, but securing the cooperation of persons in the community. This game can be fun and also provide great practice in negotiating with adults.

Let's Go Fly a Kite!

● A blustery Sunday afternoon is a perfect time to fly kites and to get a little publicity for the youth group too.

● Have the group bring their own kites, or provide materials to make kites.

● Have the players label the kites with letters to spell out the name of the youth group (example Madison Street U.M.Y.F.) and try to fly them in a row.

● Notify a local photographer to take pictures for the local paper.

● Have contests to determine the highest flying kite, the prettiest kite, the biggest kite that still flies, and so forth.

Something in Common

• Make up pairs of slips of paper with the name of the same occupation, such as lawyer, construction worker, news editor, written on both slips. The number of occupations you choose will depend on the number in your group. (If you have ten in your group, choose five occupations.)

• Give each player a slip of paper with an occupation written on it and list the following instructions on a large sheet of paper, attached to a wall:

(1) Imagine that you are at a party, looking for someone with a common interest.

(2) Circulate in the crowd, making conversation with others, until you find one other person whom you believe has the same job that you have.

(3) You are allowed to make small talk about school activities, the weather, your job, your pets, or sports, but try to get other persons to talk about matters pertaining to their occupations.

(4) You may not state the name of your occupation or ask the name of the occupation of anyone else.

(5) Simply talk about matters of interest to your profession. If you are a mechanic, tell stories about fixing cars. If you are a lawyer, talk about interesting cases.

(6) When you think you are talking to someone who has your same job, keep talking to that person until time is called.

Name Game

- Write names of famous people (living or deceased) on name tags.

- Pin these tags on the backs of participants without telling them the name.

- Have group members ask questions of one another about the identity of the person on their back.

- Only questions that may be answered with a yes or a no are allowed.

- The first person to guess the name pinned to his or her back is the winner. Keep going until all or most have identified the name.

Balloon Pop

• Divide your group in half. Each team should form single-row lines. Give each member a balloon.

• Have two counselors, officers, or even pastors face them about thirty feet away, seated in chairs.

• Play proceeds with a team member from each side bouncing a balloon with a finger and walking to one of these seated persons.

• Once there, the seated person has to get up, take the balloon, place it in the chair, and sit on it.

• When the balloon pops, the next team member proceeds in similar fashion.

• The first team to have all its balloons popped wins.

Four-Letter Words

● Give everyone a large card with one of the letters of the alphabet printed on it.

● The object is to find three other people whose letters, combined with yours, spell a four-letter word.

● Allow players one minute to form their words, and then ask each group to show the word they formed.

● Play again, forming words of five and six letters.

Foot Scramble

• Players remove their shoes and socks. With a marker, write letters of the alphabet, one per foot, on the bottom of each foot. Write a different letter on each foot.

• Give words that players will try to spell by organizing their feet.

• Very large groups can divide into teams to play this game.

Fancy Footwork

● You will need lots of smooth floor space for this activity. Each player will need a chair, newsprint, and a wide felt-tip marker.

● Ask players if they are "right-footed" or "left-footed." Then tell players to draw a picture of a church with their foot. They are to be as creative as they wish.

● Award a prize for the "fanciest footwork."

● If anyone uses his or her hand to draw a church with a footprint beside it, award a special prize for doing exactly what you asked! (Be sure to apologize for the trick!)

The Sun Rises in the East

• Seat the group in a circle. Invite players to gain wisdom by saying and doing exactly as the leader does.

• The leader leans forward, traces a large semicircle on the floor in front of his or her chair, and says: "The sun rises in the east and sets in the west."

• Everyone will be sure they know exactly how to repeat that phrase.

• The catch is that the leader, in leaning forward, rises slightly off the seat of the chair while saying: "The sun rises in the east," and settles back on the chair when saying, "and sets in the west."

• To distract the group from this basic motion, the leader might do other things such as stretch an arm before leaning forward. The leader should not repeat distracting motions or sounds each time, of course, or they will become part of the trick.

Mind Reading Stunt #1

- Based on an old Vaudeville sketch, this game keeps youth stumped for a long time.

- Pass out paper, pencils, and envelopes and ask everyone to write one question. You choose the subject.

- After they write their question, seal each one in an envelope.

- Introduce your mind reader, dressed in a turban for added effect.

- Hand the mind reader each sealed envelope. The mind reader answers each question before opening each envelope.

- Group members will be amazed as the mind reader seemingly answers their questions without opening the envelopes.

- What is the trick? The mind reader is prepared with one fictitious question and answer before the activity begins. He or she gives that fictitious answer, opens the first envelope, and recites the fictitious question. The mind reader pretends the question in the first envelope is in the second and answers it before opening the second envelope. This procedure continues until the mind reader has answered all questions. Insert a blank paper in the last envelope.

Mind Reading Stunt #2

• Choose an accomplice to perform this activity with you. Place nine magazines or books on the floor in three rows of three.

• The accomplice leaves the room as the group quietly picks one of the books on the floor.

• When your partner returns, she or he will be able to identify the book the group chose.

• One at a time, point to the books with a pointer and let your partner tell you whether or not that book is the correct one.

• The key is that the position you point to on the first book indicates the book that the group chose. (If they chose book #1, place your marker in the upper left-hand corner of the first book you select. If they chose book #5, point to the center of the first book when you ask, "Is this the one?")

• After someone indicates that he or she has figured out the formula, ask him or her to leave the room.

• Choose another book and follow the same rules to prove whether he or she has figured out this stunt.

Dictionary Game

- The idea of this game is to create definitions of unfamiliar words that will convince others that they are the real definitions.

- Materials needed are few: a dictionary, small slips of paper and pencil for each person, and a score sheet.

- The leader picks a word out of the dictionary that no one knows. The leader says the word aloud.

- The leader writes the correct definition and all other players invent and write out a possible and/or funny definition designed to sound authentic.

- All papers are folded and given to the leader who reads aloud each definition. Afterward, each player votes for the one he or she thinks is correct.

- Each player gets a point for every vote his or her definition received. Each player who guesses the correct definition also receives a point. The vote is recorded on the score sheet. The high scorer wins.

- Players take turns choosing a word from the dictionary, and the game proceeds until all have had a chance to be leaders. In a large group, several small groups can play their own game at the same time.

Musical Clothes

- This is a good game to play after a church rummage sale.

- Collect a variety of used clothing and accessories. You will need approximately five articles of clothing for each participant.

- Put all the clothing in a laundry bag or a large plastic garbage bag.

- Have the players stand in a circle.

- Play popular music. As the music plays, players are to pass the bag of clothing from one person to the next around the circle.

- When you stop the music, the person holding the bag must close his or her eyes, reach in the bag, remove one article of clothing, and put it on.

- The player who first acquires eight articles of clothing wins the game. Be sure to take pictures of the players in their new Sunday clothes and to post the photos on the church bulletin board!

Cotton Face

- This game is a variation of hot potato.

- Have players sit in a circle.

- Have a dish of hand lotion and some cotton balls (colored ones are great!) in the center of the circle.

- As music plays, everyone in the circle passes a non-food item around the circle. They cannot throw the object; they must pass it hand to hand.

- When the music stops, the person holding the object must dip a cotton ball in the hand lotion and stick the cotton ball to his or her face.

- The game continues as players fill their face with cotton balls.

Air Band Concert

• Being in an air band is like lip-synching, except that participants in an air band mimic the entire band, not just the vocalist. This is a great activity for a lock-in or an outdoor picnic.

• Suggest that the group plan an air band concert. Encourage them to invite other groups in the church to participate.

• Each air band should provide their own music and props. If you liked the air band concert, try the Music Youth Night!

Music Youth Night

• Gather cassette tapes of popular contemporary Christian music and several tape players. (Each group will need its own tape player.)

• Recruit volunteers to bring videotaping equipment and to tape the individual concerts.

• At the beginning of the recreation period, form groups of five to seven people.

• Allow each group to select a song for a music video performance. Give the groups a thirty-minute time limit for rehearsal and for the actual performance.

• Have a TV and VCR set up in order to replay the videos after they are finished.

Youth Fellowship Trivia

● Make up a pool of questions from experiences you've had as a youth group and test yourselves. Besides the fun of competition, you'll share some laughter and some memories worth rediscovering and keeping.

● Divide your group into teams of twos or threes.

● Give teams these instructions: "Come up with twenty questions (more or less depending on the size of the group and the amount of time you have to spend) about experiences we've had together as a youth group."

● Make sure the questions you ask could be answered by anyone who was present when the event happened.

● When teams have finished their question lists, ask your adult leader to be scorekeeper.

● Have team 1 ask each other team a question. If a team answers correctly, they score ten points. If not, other teams (except for the questioners) get a chance to answer.

● Only one team can score points on a question.

● You can end the game at any time when both sides have had an equal number of questions.

Youth Feud

- This game is patterned after the television show Family Feud. Poll the adult Sunday school classes in your church.

- Prepare a question sheet to distribute to the adults in the congregation. The questions asked should be general such as: "Name five Old Testament characters; name four books in the New Testament; name five of the apostles; name five of the Ten Commandments."

- Collect the response sheets and tally the answers. Select the top five or six vote-getters in each category as the answers for the game.

- Form two teams and have the teams sit in straight lines across from one another.

- The first persons in line on each team face off. The first one to answer the question controls the question and their teammates choose to take the question or pass. Each team member in turn is asked for a survey answer.

- Each team is allowed three wrong answers and then the other team gets a chance to steal. In a successful "steal" the team scores for each correct answer their opponents had already given for that question.

- For the second question, the second persons in line face off and so on down the line until everyone has had a chance to participate in the game.

STRICTLY QUIET

INTRODUCTION

Anything for a Quiet Life.
Thomas Middleton, Title of play, 1662

Here is a section for the quieter moments in your youth group. Use these games to "cool down" after other, more rigorous games, to wind down a meeting, to keep you going the last one hundred miles in a church van, or in the wee hours of the morning during a lock-in retreat. All of these are guaranteed to enrich your group's more mellow moments.

Ice Melt

● Make a block of ice by filling a half-gallon milk carton or jug with water and freezing it.

● Cut away the carton or jug and place the block of ice on a sidewalk or church parking lot.

● Each person should write down what time he or she thinks it will be when the ice is completely melted.

● You may want to do a trial run so that you have an idea of how long it will take. It takes longer than you think! You can also use a smaller ice block.

● Assign players turns watching the ice melt and to announce the time it is completely melted.

● Give a glass of iced tea or ice cube trophy to the person who came closest to guessing the "meltdown."

A What?

● Have everyone sit in a circle for this game.

● Begin by passing a cup (or other object) to the right.

● Say to the person sitting on your right, "This is a cup." That person responds by saying, "A what?" and you answer, "A cup." He or she then hands the cup to the next person in the circle and says, "This is a cup." That person asks, "A what?" The second person turns to you and repeats the question, saying, "A what?" You say, "A cup," the person on your right says, "A cup," and the third person takes the cup to the fourth person in the circle. Continue around the circle.

● To make the game more difficult, pass a second object to the left.

● It is fun when the two objects meet in the circle. Continue until both objects reach the person who started the game.

● For greater challenge and to use this game to review the first names in your group, begin by saying, "My name is Debra and this is a cup." The second person can ask, "A what?" " A cup."

● When passing the cup from the second person to the third, he or she says, "My name is Cris and Debra says that this is a cup." Continue to mention names. "My name is Keith and Cris says that Debra says that this is a cup." Fun and confusion results!

Chewing Gum Sculpture

● Give group members a piece of bubble gum, two or three toothpicks, and an index card.

● The object is to create a sculpture using those items.

● After the creations have been completed, ask individuals to explain each sculpture.

Drawing With the Other Side of Someone's Brain

- Form teams of two.

- Give one player in each pair a simple design, such as a stop sign with an X drawn through it or the letter Z with two horizontal lines of different lengths drawn through it. The design should be simple, but also difficult to describe.

- Give the other player in each pair a sheet of paper and a pencil.

- The first player will tell the second player how to draw the design. When his or her directions are complete, the second player has one minute to draw the design. He or she may not ask questions or clarify directions.

- After one minute, have teammates compare their designs.

- Then ask the teammates to reverse roles, give each pair a new design, and play again. This time, allow the "artist" to ask questions for clarification. The player describing the design may answer as completely as possible without showing the design.

- Discuss which way worked better. What does this teach us about communication?

Slide Stories

● Bring some slides to your group meeting. If possible, choose some activity pictures featuring members of your group.

● Divide the group into small teams of two or more.

● Give each team eight to fifteen slides and instruct them to place the pictures in any order they choose. They should create a story based on that order.

● After ten minutes of creative work, bring the teams back into a total group, provide a slide projector, and give each team a chance to tell their story to the rest of the group.

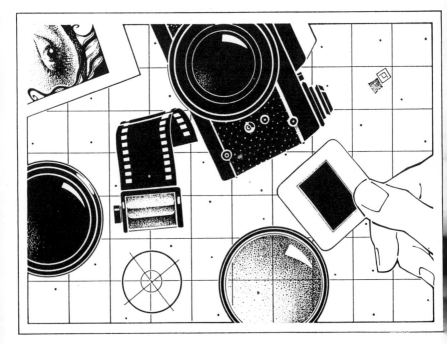

Continuous Story

● This activity will encourage teamwork and creativity. Ask one person to create a story.

● Use people from your group as characters or make the story entirely fictitious.

● Encourage the storyteller to expand the plot within a time limit of one minute.

● At the end of one minute, the next person continues the story, adding characters and plot.

● Continue in this manner, giving each person a minute to create part of the story. The results can be hilarious!

One-Minute Talk

• Select three volunteers to compete against one another for a worthwhile prize (such as a UMYF T-shirt.) Their job is to talk for one minute without seeing a clock or having someone call time.

• Assign a topic, such as your youth group mission trip or an event in their school.

• Recruit an official timekeeper to record the exact length of the talk. All times are confidential until the end.

• Let each person speak one at a time. After all three youth have spoken, award the prize to the person who came closest to speaking for exactly one minute.

Afterglow Event

• Afterglow events warm the heart and strengthen the bonds of a group. Many youth groups hold them once a month, following a regular meeting.

• Afterglows are a time when groups bring out the guitars, Christian tapes or songbooks, Bibles, and so on and enjoy conversation, music, and prayer together.

• While recreation "loosens" a group and serves, in part, to initiate intimacy, afterglow events deepen intimacy and strengthen Christian bonds.